1

Parents Orators Writers Artists Readers

P.o.w.a.r

A Family Learning Project.

Other books from the Powar series include the Intermediate Reader, 'Weeding Cane', the Beginner Reader, 'Learn to Listen, Then You Won't Feel' and the anthology 'The Power From Within'. Please check the back of this book for details of the Powar Poster Collection.

Our Say

Parents rapping about life, parenthood and their children

NATIONAL
LOTTERY
CHARITIES
BOARD

Powar Project Co-ordinator, Leroy Williamson
Crèche Co-ordinator, Elizabeth Aryee
Text copyright © Anita Allen, Elizabeth Henry, Sonia Hughes, Paulette Martin. 2001
Editor, Leroy Williamson
Illustrations, Ian Bobb
Design, Ian Bobb and Leroy Williamson

Published & distributed by Gatehouse Books Ltd.
Hulme Adult Education Centre, Stretford Road, Manchester M15 5FQ.
Printed by RAP Ltd, Clock Street, Hollinwood, Oldham, OL9 7LY
ISBN 0 906253 86 1
British Library cataloguing in publication data:
A catalogue record for this book is available from the British Library

'Our Say' was developed from writing originally produced by Anita Allen, Elizabeth Henry,
Sonia Hughes and Paulette Martin with editor, Leroy Williamson.
The writing was drawn from workshops during the Powar family learning project at
Claremont Infant School, Moss Side, Manchester.

One Gatehouse reading circle recommended these stories for publication. Many
thanks for their work to Steph Prior, Sonia Hammond, Susan Armstrong, Wendy
Gibbons, Monica Ebanks and Joseph Campbell.

Thanks also to the English and basic skills groups run by Manchester Adult Education
Services at Ducie Adult Education Centre and Greenheys Adult Education Centre with
whom we piloted a first draft of this book.

Special thanks also to Judy Craven, Sonia Hammond, Ruth Nunes, Harvey Nisbett and
Pat Lee who were instrumental to the success of the project.

Gatehouse acknowledges grant aid towards the production of this book from The
National Lottery and Manchester City Council.

Gatehouse is a member of The Federation of Worker Writers & Community Publishers.

Gatehouse provides an opportunity for writers to express their thoughts and feelings
on aspects of their lives. The views expressed are not necessarily those of Gatehouse.

Contents

Preface

Family Literacy

Family literacy is all about parents and children learning together and from each other, given that parents are the first and most important teachers a child can have. Family literacy programmes aim to create awareness amongst parents of how and what children are taught within school. They also demonstrate ways in which parents can help their child with reading and writing and in turn gain confidence with their own literacy skills.

Parental support is key to the success or failure of many of our children. Especially in a growing climate of high exclusion rates, limited resources, big class sizes and intense social and peer pressures.

Powar   *P.arents O.rators W.riters A.rtists R.eaders*

The Powar Family Learning Project was launched at Claremont Infant School, Moss Side Manchester in 1999 Its aim was to deliver a programme that would benefit parents of children of African descent. A key objective is to encourage parents to express themselves. Powar aims to empower by developing parents' talents as orators, writers, artists and readers. The writing in this book represents the first fruits of this labour.

This and the accompanying books in the Powar Series have been drawn from a parents' writing group at Claremont Infant School. We met for weekly workshops for over a year. Workshops used an African and African-Caribbean cultural perspective at its core and included sessions on oral story telling, music therapy, puppet making and black literature. These workshops were complemented by sessions on school procedures, the National Curriculum and practical support activities that could be done at home with children.

The Writing

The other half of the project involved getting parents to write. As editor of the project, it was my job to encourage parents to write. Many of the parents had not written anything creative for a long time, since school, for some. Subsequently, confidence and self-belief to express in their own voice was lacking at the beginning. However, after the first workshops, the parents grew to know each other quite well. We gained each other's trust and respect and gelled together as a group. Sometimes it was like sitting in the midst of long lost sisters who had just been reunited and had a lot of catching up to do.

Early on, we found that a good method to extract writing from the group was first to have a discussion workshop about an issue or opinion. All workshops were tape recorded and then transcribed. The transcribed notes were then presented to the parents with suggestions and advice on how to complete a writing exercise.

In these early sessions, we talked, debated and reasoned about issues related to being a parent and being a parent of a black child. We covered a range of issues such as concepts of freedom, identity, role models, fears and hopes and parenting values. The wealth of writing that came from this approach was inspired first and foremost by the children. The children more than anything else were the driving force behind the parents' writing. However, I feel that if the parents were not given time and space to express themselves orally in the first instance, then the richness and honesty of the writing may not have shone through like it does.

For myself as the co-ordinator and editor of the project the time spent with the group has been enjoyable, rewarding, testing but above all, an enlightening adventure.

So therefore, maximum respect to the writers - Anita Allen, Paulette Martin, Sonia Hughes and Elizabeth Henry. And also to their children and grandchildren who kept us all on our toes - Solomon, Erika and Jaimeel, Luke and Isaac, Nathanael and Kerith.

What makes this collection of writing so special is that each parent offers a distinctive and original voice but all seem to connect at the same root. The writing therefore may hold a special meaning for everybody, if not only for parents. We hope you enjoy reading the books and trust you will be able to take something positive from them.

Leroy Williamson
(Editor)

Introduction

This book was written with much dedication by some of the parents and carers of children who attend Claremont Infant School. Parents have displayed their dedication in many, many ways, particularly to their children, so it isn't surprising to see that they could produce such quality literature.

Patricia Lee, Head Teacher, and Ruth Nunes, a teacher at the school who supports families of African descent, have endeavoured over the years to involve parents at every level of their children's education. They believe that parents are the real experts. Leroy Williamson, the project co-ordinator, has shown strength of spirit and has encouraged the women in the group, inspiring and helping to build the confidence required to realise their full potential.

As a child, I often heard the saying, 'women are the weaker sex.' But this, as the years have passed, has proved to be more and more untrue. Weakness and strength like many others words can be defined in a million different ways by a million different people. On reaching adulthood I began to realise that we can only reach true definitions when we base them on what we have within. Only when we look within, do we find real truth and meaning in the outside world. Parents, on the whole, pass on to their children the values and survival skills that they feel their children should possess. They know that we all have to look into ourselves, at what we have been given, to make sense of our world. Mothers and fathers both play their roles in this process in their own unique but yet similar ways. As far as I have experienced, women have shown themselves to be capable of directing the play of life with a show of strength beyond measure.

The women who created this amazing writing set out at the beginning to keep it real. They have written of their hopes, dreams, fears, loves and hates, candidly, which will surely move the soul of anyone who reads. Freedom and security for their children is one of the themes running through these pieces. Look beyond the surface and see how women through the ages past, present and future have held these concerns close to their hearts, weaving those concepts into their active lives.

Reading this book and other books in the Powar series involves the reader viewing life from a range of experiences, through the eyes of a child, sister, partner or wife and mother. The authors have succeeded in producing something that can be felt, seen with the mind's eye and almost touched. The power of this literature is such that the experiences of these parents become 'real' and meaningful to readers of any background.

Harvey Nisbett
(Local teacher who works with ethnic minority children at Claremont School)

Who Am I?

Who am I?   *Who you are is the sum of your past, present and hopes for the future.*

There is an old saying that you can know somebody all your life and not really know them.   But I often ask, do we really truly know ourselves?   Writing about oneself is not the same as talking about oneself. Maybe this is because writing allows us to explore the sum of our parts in more depth.

The writing that follows is drawn from a workshop where the group drew a series of sketches that relate to a key moment or event in their life. Everybody then explained what their *stick drawing* was supposed to be, and also what it represented. This approach allowed for a frank, and honest discussion, where personal experiences became shared experiences.

It's Where I'm From and Where I'm At.

by Sonia Hughes.

It's Where I'm From and Where I'm At

The thing about my life -
it's mostly been a straight line
there are no major dips
there are no terrific highs
mainly a constant hum
sometimes a sigh.

Born
Started a happy chocolate child 'cept I wished my hair
could swish and none of the boys wanted to chase me to
kiss my black lips.   But I was happy nonetheless, put on
plays, spent the days in the park.

My brother died
Became a disgruntled, deep and philosophical teenager
who read books whose meaning I didn't understand, but I
read them just the same.

Moved to London
Now a rebel soldier, reading Marx and doing time. Standing on the barricades, squatting in the East End, emancipating workers, defending prisoners of the uprisings, liberating Africa and getting laid.

Got a job
Hail the yuppie without the finance, nothing less than leather-soled shoes. I partied, did lunch, drank spritzers, shopped, read glossies, worked out, lost my fire, squashed my dreams.

Went to the Caribbean
Ditched all my white folks. Clung to my black folks. Heard about the old God.   Listened to my heartbeat. Searched for a meaning, couldn't find one so drank Canei and partied harder still.

Travelled to Africa
Discovered the old God, revelled in my homecoming, felt my true heartbeat, plugged into my dignity. Came back with head high, back straight and belly full.

Became a mummy
Knew the real meaning, wondered at the wondrous.
Kissed my baby's pearly toes, lost myself to motherhood,
ate Mars bars and digestives, and prayed for lots more
time.

Went to university
Stretched the possibilities, questioned my potential,
gathered terminology, regained my ambition, tested my
virtuosity, compromised my motherhood.

And now
Looking for the next step, maybe love, maybe money,
maybe science, maybe God, maybe England, maybe
elsewhere, maybe houses, maybe mountains, lots of ifs
and whens and buts.

My Life In a Nutshell.

by Anita Allen

My Life in a Nutshell

I always wanted to be old enough
To do as I please.
Then one day I got lucky, I was free.
It didn't last long, I didn't handle it right.
For number one came, A she was called,
Followed by B who almost took my breath away.
C came along, now I'm frustrated as hell.
Then D came and challenged me to be a mother of four.

Alone, jobless, frustrated, with no real friends,
I walked with a curve for my stomach always aches.
Washing, cooking, cleaning, nibbling
And sewing for four.
My days never end till a quarter to four.

Lying down tired, frustrated, not bored,
For all four would come hiding behind the door.
Then we would read and tell stories with happy endings.
I would dream of the day ours would end happily too.

I got a job doing electronics all day.
Evenings I'd do my chores.
Just before bedtime, we'd pray.
Next morning as I got ready for another hectic day,
I was so happy to see my children smiling away!

Looking back I realise how very childish I was.
I've grown now, but all through the way,
We've learned from each other.
My A, B, C and D have made me so proud.
They've taught me so much.
So now I've got E,
With my Gran's initials
J, O, and little C.

3D Through the Third Eye.

by Elizabeth Henry.

3D through the 3rd Eye

Death   Deliverance   Determination

If I tried to write about my life it would be a book the size *of War and Peace.* So I decided to select three things that I believe have in some way made me who I am today and have influenced the way I think today. The fact that I have chosen one person and two experiences does not mean that what I have omitted is forgotten or unimportant. I believe that every detail of one's life should be cherished because that is what makes the individual.

Let me tell you about me. As a very small child I would say that my life consisted of trees, fields, and wide-open spaces. I was also allowed to roam as long as I returned for meals. Society seemed different then. For all my freedom, the place I chose to frequent was my Nana and Grandad's house.

We called them Nin and Pop. Nin always baked lovely cakes, played games with us and listened. Pop spent his time in his immaculate garden. He also had a greenhouse and even now, whenever I smell homegrown tomatoes, I think of Pop. It was Pop who died first; my first experience of death. I got through it with Nin's help. She moved to a flat just a street away from the house and life continued. She missed Pop.

Nin was always there to help others. She was always willing to give people a chance. No matter what difficulties she had to face, Nin always smiled. Nin was a teacher although I do not think that was her intention. She did not teach English or Maths in school. She taught patience, understanding and compassion - priceless life skills. I cried a lot when she died. However I know she is now being rewarded.

I never thought that you would go
without any warning or clue.
I thought you'd be here forever,
if only that were true.
As always, you knew best,
you knew the time was right.
To us it was the saddest day
when you were taken from our sight.
For God gave you back your husband,
but took away this life.
Giving you both eternal happiness,
together as loving husband and wife.

At the age of twenty-eight I changed my life dramatically.
I was buying a house, my parents lived with me. I had a
good job which could have been a career for life. I had a
car and just about anything else I thought I needed.
One day, for no apparent reason, I was devastated by
depression. My life fell apart. I could not function as I
had done before. No one including myself could
understand why. The answer to that I still do not know.

Six months of my life were shrouded with total darkness.
One day I was coming home from yet another doctor's
appointment. I stood waiting on the station platform.
I could see the train approaching. I knew I was going
under it. I felt beaten, trapped and ashamed. I did not
consider how many lives would change because of my
actions. I just could not take any more.

The train was closer. Then a child of about three ran
towards me, stopped just out of reach and laughed. One
rational thought came to my mind, this child should not
be alone on the platform. The child giggled and smiled.
The train pulled into the station and stopped. The child
skipped away out of sight never getting on the train.
I went home and, day by day, got myself out of the state
of depression. I made a lot of decisions about my life.

I sold my house and car and moved to Manchester.
I know one thing - that child saved my life.

Living life as lies
the woman slowly crumbles,
as through the mine-filled world
alone, afraid, she stumbles.
Disregarding all the signs
friends and family pass her by,
all surroundings disengage
and inner strength just dies.
Will she ever return to life
without the lies and fears,
or will this lonely woman
drown in her own tears?
She wants to reach for help
not give in to the sorrow,
but even she needs someone
to help her through tomorrow.

Now I live a very different kind of life, well in the materialistic sense, anyway. Moving to Manchester opened my eyes. I came here with nothing.

I used the money from the sale of the house and car to buy my mum and dad somewhere of their choice to live.

I did some voluntary work and claimed social security. My first visit to claim was a mind-blowing experience. Most of the people waiting were rude and abusive to the people behind the counters. One man picked up a chair and tried to smash the glass divide. One woman was crying, sobbing, "What am I supposed to do?" I had gone from being well off to having nothing, and I was now witnessing what can happen when you live with nothing for a long time.

I've lived on both sides of the street.

Once when I wanted something, I bought it. I've been so poor that I have fed my children and starved myself. Now I would say that I am in the middle. I like it here. For as long as I live, I will always have the two most valuable things, my faith and my family. Everything else comes and goes. So who knows what the rest of my life has in store? I'm waiting.

From day to day
the only way to survive,
waiting in pain
for the giro to arrive.
The kids are dirty
their clothes are worn.
She is starving
her heart is torn.
Where's the next meal
with no money in the purse?
Getting into debt,
loan-sharks making it worse.
No money for heat,
food or light.
Officials with comforts
say be legal and right.
Some tell her work,
don't put in your card,
steal or beg,
things won't be so hard.
She does not want riches
just food for her kin.
But in these social climes
       surviving is a sin.

The Place I Call Home

by Anita Allen

The Place I Call Home

I came to England because of the ongoing volcanic crisis on my island. Since coming to England, I have become secretly envious when people talk about going home on holiday. When I think of my island, I have growing fears inside me. My greatest fear is that my island was possibly created by a volcano, and could very well be destroyed by it. So now my fear raises questions within me. Haunting questions like -

Will my island still be there when the crisis is over?
Will I ever be able to go back home even for a visit?
Or will I be one of those folks without an island to identify with?

I feel so scared just thinking about it, that it sometimes hurts.

One night while watching the news I saw the elderly of China in Disneyland having fun with my favourite Disney characters. There was Mickey, Mini, Goofy and even Barney, my favourite. I was so happy for them, I decided to make plans to go to visit my sister in Florida. Then visit Disney myself. A week later, the idea wasn't appealing.

So my plans went out the door.

I then started to think it would be nice to go to Africa and visit the places where my ancestors are from. That idea didn't even materialise. I felt so depressed and hopeless that I would stay here in Manchester and die without seeing any other place, much less home. Then on Monday night, it happened. I saw a documentary on Montserrat and its volcano. I knew without a doubt that home was in fact my destiny. I knew that no other place could do anything for me at this time. Even though things won't ever be the same, it will always be the place of my roots and culture.

Montserrat, also known as the Emerald Isle, is a small island in the Caribbean Sea. It is known for its saw-tooth mountains and friendly people. It was 39.6 square miles with beautiful black sand beaches and one white sand beach. The population was approximately 12,000 and our houses sat brightly upon the hills with every imaginable colour you can think of. Our water comes from the springs in the mountain and our main dishes are goat water and mountain chicken. Our national flower is the Heliconia and the national bird is the Oriole.

The volcano started erupting on July 18th 1995. The

ongoing crisis of the volcano has disrupted our lives and three quarters of the island is unsafe to live on. About half of it is burnt out or covered with ash, mud flows and pyroclastic flows[1].

Many people have left for one reason or the other. If I put aside my real reason for leaving, I could envy those who are left behind. I would go to the Montserrat that I knew, not Disneyland or Florida. Not even my fascination with going to Africa could give me the inner peace and joy I would feel if I did go home.

I would love to see my children and grandchildren that I left behind. Phonecalls are so expensive but sometimes I just have to call and fill in this emptiness. I miss having a fresh mango, guava, cherry or plum, in fact, fruits of all seasons. Then there's the sunshine, the walk on the beach, the occasional drink with friends.

Gazing at the dome and the constant puffing of the ash clouds makes me think, what is the next move and what is the fate of our island? I would rather wander around villages trying to figure what was here or there, even the

---

[1] A dense mass of very hot ash, lava fragments, and gases ejected explosively from a volcano and often flowing at great speed.

forbidden yards, but especially the one with the sign that reads, "Beware of the dogs, but the owner bites harder."

I would like to see a few ash clouds and even a pyroclastic flow bubbling down the mountain, just like billions of oversized cauliflowers. I would like to see the volcano glowing in the night when it is not steaming too much. It is like fireworks on the Fourth of July in America, only its red and gold decorating the mountain side. It's one of the most beautiful sights I've ever seen, but deadly.

I know things will not be the same again and lives have been changed, some shortened, others readjusted. Our prayer is that God would continue to be in control and would spare our island and those that remain. So we can have a place to call home, even if we don't go back.

Old Rip Van Winkle

by Anita Allen

Old Rip Van Winkle

We were a comfortable people
Caring, sharing, hating, and loving,
High-spirited, carefree but godly,
Enjoying the best life had to offer,
Thinking disaster belonged to someone else,
And then one night he came.

Old Rip Van Winkle who was dormant on the hills
Awoke one day and started puffing smoke,
Then made his mighty rumbling roar
Grinding the rocks beneath the earth.
Then mud flows, pyroclastic flows,
Ash clouds reaching thousands of miles
Bringing lightning and thunder from the skies,
Making the little emerald isle
As grey as grey can be.
He had taken over.

He grew like nothing else I've ever seen,
Stood like a giant up on the mountain top
Cracking the hills and mountains, pushing them away.

The people scattered like dumb, driven cattle,
Driven like the ash clouds,
To places formerly unknown.

A Femme Fatale

by Paulette Hastin

Femme Fatale - A Woman's Work

Foreword

Femme Fatale – A Woman's Work was conceived from a collection of memories I had as I was growing up and the ideals taught me about how I should behave as a young lady.

It describes also the way I felt. It was assumed that women be a certain way and men another, and that it was not a problem that men do not know anything of domesticity. The end of the poem is a liberated announcement of a changing world for women.

I wrote this poem to the tune of *Tom's Diner* by Suzanne Vega.

Femme Fatale - A Woman's Work

I was standing in the kitchen
With my hands inside a chicken
My mum said I had to do it
All because I was a woman
And I turned around and faced her
Whilst my hands became all bloody
And I heard my little brother
Running quick to the front door.

I remember I was taunted
Just because I couldn't get it
Was it really so important
That I learned to cook and clean up
For the older I have grown
And seen the young boys turn to old men
Your attitudes are changing
And it's their turn to dry the plates.

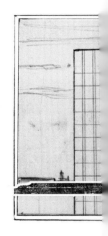

Meanwhile home is still the kitchen
Yes that's me cleaning the chicken

My mum brought me up to do it
'Cos she knows that we are women
And I hear the sound of footsteps
As I swivel round to face him
And my son he gets the message
And he's already out the door.

Oh it's time to don the trousers
Iron out all age old creases
As I sit behind the big desk
In my board directors room.

Our Children, The Future

Children represent the seeds from which hope grows. Like young plants children need strong roots, a good diet and a conducive environment. If children are to grow healthy and strong they also need guidance, protection and to be loved unconditionally.

The path from birth to adulthood is a lot different now than for the previous generations. Children are growing up faster, some say too fast. In today's ever changing world children seem to be directly in the firing line, taking more than their fair share of blame for society's problems.

In the following pieces, parents have written letters to their children for them to open in the future. In the letters the parents talk candidly about their hopes and fears and try to explain the difficulties they face as parents.

We Three

by Elizabeth Henry

We Three

235 Wheldon Street,
Moss Side,
Manchester.

Hi, my mates, Luke and Isaac,

I often wonder how you will recall your childhood. When there was the two of you and I was the only parent, I set myself some guidelines - teach not preach, steer not push. I would not say that I always got it right, still I tried.

I always wanted to try and teach you what I would class as the fundamental things in life in the hope that I could try and make your lives simpler. I believe that knowledge is the key to many things; freedom, security, education and choice. From these basic things I hoped that you could learn to deal with what life 'throws' at you and that you would be able to understand your true selves.

If there was one thing that I knew all through my life, it was that things are not always easy. When you were both growing up, I had to expect that you would encounter racism. That is a sad thing to say. However, I do not believe that such a destructive emotion will be eradicated in your lifetime. I would look at you both and know that you would be treated differently by some, purely based on your looks. How could I prepare you for the offensive behaviour of others?

We live in what is classed as a multicultural society. That to me means that people live together who are from varied cultures and everyone should respect what that entails. Culture to me is no more than habits that we are brought up with, such as different tastes in music, food or religious beliefs. They are what make us who we are and should not be used as a weapon to browbeat one another. Without culture one has no roots and no sense of identity from which we can start to build a personality, a life.

When you look in the mirror, do not see the names that others may call you. Never believe that you are in any way beneath others because of how you look. If you can look in the mirror and know that you are not a bad person, hold your head high and rise above the insanity of racism.

I always hoped to give you the type of childhood that I remember having. However, because of society and the personal problems we had, that was not to be. When I was young, doors were never locked. Children had many adults who were 'aunties' and 'uncles' to them. The streets were a reasonably safe place to play. That is not the case now. When you were young, some of your friends' parents would allow them to go and play on the streets all day, wander off to the parks and not be concerned that they were out of sight.

I am sure that at times you hated me because I would not give you that same freedom. It was just that I did not want either or both of you to become a statistic, another child killed on a busy road or abducted, even murdered. I also did not want you to feel stifled. I always felt that I was walking a tightrope. If I took a chance and gave you too much freedom, I could have lost you forever. If I lessened your freedom, you might despise me and turn away from me. At least then there would be a chance that you could grow up and begin to understand why. At least then, you could come back.

I tried to teach you that freedom and security are not only gained through materialism. We never had a lot of money. I saw that as a godsend. I could tell you and show you that money, although a necessity is also a great weapon used to trap and enslave people. Luke and Isaac, when you only believe in money as a way to enrich your lives, you are setting the stage for your own downfall.

Freedom and security come from within. Without faith, the struggle to attain these things becomes greater. When you have a rich life, you have family, good friends but most importantly, you are strong internally. Some will seek to destroy that, simply because of jealousy. Materialism is neither freedom nor security. It can be a fast track to destruction on a mental, physical and spiritual level.

When I wrote this letter Luke, you were only seven, Isaac just five. Yet even at those ages I was so impressed with the way you dealt with life's ups and downs. Your smiles were always an inspiration. When you laughed, it was music to my ears.

The best freedom that I can offer you both is to teach you

that you are both important. You have value in the multitude of things that you have to offer, no matter how small they may seem. The best security I can give you is showing you that my love is unconditional and will never waver. Whatever paths you choose in your lives, I will always be there in whatever capacity you may need me.

Only ever be beholden to your Creator. Whatever choices you have to make in your lives, use one rule: if you can face God and not be ashamed, then it will be the right choice.

My Love Always

Mum.

Its All Up To You

by Sonia Hughes.

It's All Up To You

Number 1
Peace of Mind Street,
Livesville.

Dear Solomon,

I have lived just thirty three years and over time, experience and learning from my life and the life of others, I have gathered some scraps of knowledge. And if you believe me, if you trust me, I can tell you what I've learnt in the next five hundred words. For those five hundred words are as little and as much as I know for sure.

A state of constant happiness is what people seem to strive for and believe is theirs as of right. It's not, and it's an illusion. But you can reach a relative state of contentment and satisfaction if you create your own freedom and build your own security.

Freedom and security - they can be contradictory and mutually exclusive. But if you get to know them well, security will give you freedom, and freedom will bring you security.

What is freedom and security?

Well the way I see it;
Freedom is the absence of constraints.

Security is the belief that no matter how far you fall, or how hurt you are that you will emerge on the other side, bruised maybe, but wiser.

Constraints are external or self-imposed. Few are physical, some are legal, most are socially constructed, but the ones that bind you tightest are those contrived in your own head. Free yourself from the latter and all the others will fall away as shackles turning to dust.

People will only have power over you, if you give it to them.
Hold your power, know your power, carve your freedom.
Make your place free.
Even in the most confined of spaces, George, Nelson, Bobby [1] all say,

"Emancipate your mind, liberate your soul."

---

[1] George Jackson, Nelson Mandela and Bobby Sands were all political prisoners.

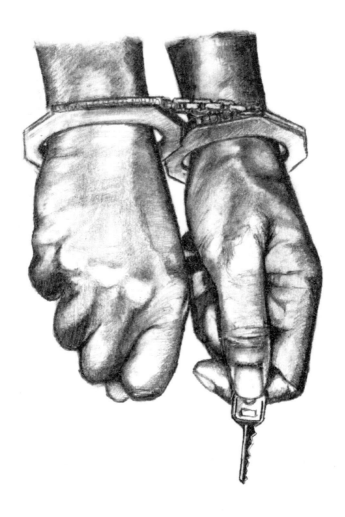

Easily said, rarely done. To free your mind there has to be self belief, self worth, self knowledge that takes so much time, so much experience. You have to allow yourself to walk on precipices many times to achieve those.

That takes security. I love you. But it needs more than that even as strong and as deep and as long as my love is. You need more. So that you don't wait for anyone, so you can strike out on your own, so that rejection and failure cannot slay you, so you are not always afraid.

And things will scare you in your life, bigger than the invisible monster that lurks at the top of the dark stairs now. Your own private fears, your self doubts, these will hold you back. How to fight these I don't really know. But if you're aware the monsters are out there, that at least is a defence against any surprise attack. You can begin to build your own defences before they pounce, and they will.

Nobody but you can provide you with security.
You must know yourself
You must grow yourself
Learn to trust yourself.

People you love will come and go, even me, and you will
remain. So make yourself your blanket, wrap yourself in
your love, huddle with yourself to create warmth.
Take comfort in the fact that others have gone this way
before and more will follow. But be wise to the truth that
"You one born and you one a go dead."

Are these lessons about freedom and security more im-
portant than any other of life's lessons? Solomon, I don't
know, but they hold within them essentials, of love, peace
of mind, courage, integrity, trust and once again love.

It's all up to you, Baby

More and more love,

Mummy

Our Say

by Paulette Martin.

Our Say

Foreword

In a world where children are so much more vulnerable physically, mentally and spiritually, I do not feel comfortable exposing my love and protection for them to anyone. I have produced a poem which I hope will ask the question and leave you to answer what freedom and security means to you, for your own children, whilst saying a little of what it means to me.

Our Say

A letter to say and explain at best
The trials, tribulations, humiliations and tests
What we wanted to give?
What we wanted to show?
That love never changes wherever you go.

To give you a basis and foundation firm
Our faith in the Bible and your growth in the Lord
Our role as your parents
Our efforts well tried.
Dreams and hopes for the future
With honesty as your guide.

Why we had to teach you which way you should go,
Why some things we held from you,
Why some things we said, no.
Why your faith was important,
Why the stories showed clear, the examples of faith,
That we hold so dear.

Why we kept a Sabbath when others said, why?
The parties you missed and the tear sometimes cried,
Of our reasons for keeping these special times
Far and knowing, the Lord has to come before all.
Your happiness when it all became clear,
When a prayer that you whispered was answered and said,
How glad that you were that you said a few words!
That you helped catch a killer
Of a life spared on earth.

A letter to say that a freedom once had
No longer was like when me and your Dad
Grew up with open doors
And keys hanging from letter boxes
Going in and out of each other's houses.
But because of the fear and dread
Walking or driving you to school instead
Was a necessity, a thing to be done.

We had no other choice we wanted no harm,
No news delivered by TV or police
That a child has gone missing when playing on the street.
Security is no longer being left with a friend
As the friend could suddenly be at the end
Of a life, of a child or a rape of a girl
Of a snatch from a playground
As the day closes in.

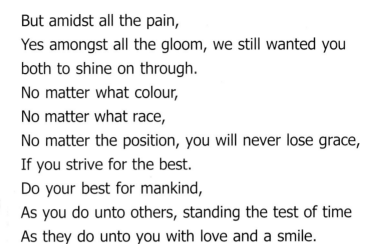

But amidst all the pain,
Yes amongst all the gloom, we still wanted you
both to shine on through.
No matter what colour,
No matter what race,
No matter the position, you will never lose grace,
If you strive for the best.
Do your best for mankind,
As you do unto others, standing the test of time
As they do unto you with love and a smile.

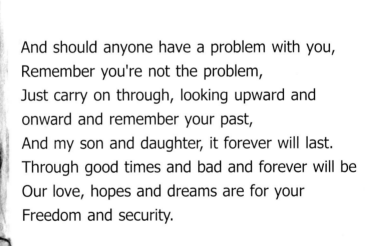

And should anyone have a problem with you,
Remember you're not the problem,
Just carry on through, looking upward and
onward and remember your past,
And my son and daughter, it forever will last.
Through good times and bad and forever will be
Our love, hopes and dreams are for your
Freedom and security.

"To My Daughter

by Anita Allen.

To My Daughter

Flemmings Village,
Salem,
Montserrat.

Dear Daughter,

Life is full of obstacles but there are two words I would like to talk to you about. They are freedom and security. These are very simple words, often spoken. They can be very powerful in the making or the breaking of a person. So always remember who you are and where you come from, so that you'll be better able to know where you are going.

Coming into this world, one could easily think or even shout out, "I'm free." I would like to say yes, but I can't because life is full of boundaries. So whatever freedom or security we allow ourselves has to come from deep within.

Our ancestors were sold as slaves and brought out of Africa into the Western world, to a place they knew nothing of. They were driven and humiliated to their very lowest. Separated from their family, friends and language, they had to come together in unity to fight for their freedom. This was later given to them in a very small way. They were able to celebrate with the only thing they had brought with them, their culture.

Much later we entered into another phase of life. We were asked to come and help rebuild Britain after the war. Humiliation at another level began. We were spat upon, called names and even burned alive in our homes because of racism. We were treated like Caribbean dogs without an owner.

Many people's loss was very great, many lost the will to go on. Many lost themselves, yet many are still fighting and hoping.

For instance, the parents of a young lad Stephen Lawrence are fighting for justice for their son who was brutally murdered in 1993. No one has been officially charged with his murder. Yet they have been fighting not only for Stephen but for the many more blacks who have died in a similar manner. They haven't got justice but they have been heard, which in itself is an achievement.

Strength, perseverance, courage and love have brought us this far. We are here today as free as we are, or allow ourselves to be, at a price, a very high price. I guess you have to be strong and motivated from within, be assertive so you can ensure you say and do the right thing.

As a child, I wanted my freedom so bad I dreamt of being on my own. When the time came and I was truly free, I was so free that I blew it. So I began wondering, why is it we can't value freedom? And is there any way possible our children and grandchildren can handle freedom positively?

Some of the obstacles you may meet on the way are:

1 *Prejudice: it could be easy if you know how to deal with it. You have to have confidence in yourself always. Have a good knowledge of your roots and culture. Be observant, learn as much as you can. There is no mountain too high for you to climb.*

2 *Peer pressure: this is a very dangerous one. Again it has everything to do with believing in yourself and having that confidence. You don't always have to do what your friends are doing. A true friend would love and respect you, no matter what. One person can make a difference. Stand up for what you believe in.*

3 *Drugs: the devil's lethal weapon.*
You can be whatever you want to be without any help from powder, grass or pills.

Spiritually, God has been good to us as a family. There is a book full of stories for all who could read them or listen. Read it my child, you'll find knowledge, wisdom and understanding. Speak if you ever feel the need, someone will listen. For even the dull and ignorant have a story to tell.

I know you dislike lots of things I do and say. I know at times you feel I embarrass you. I am very sorry. I hope one day though, you're able to understand why I did some of the things you thought were so wrong and perhaps forgive me. I am not saying I'm always right.

Do you remember the party you were invited to and you wanted to go as some special person or thing? I dressed you as my princess and when you got there everyone else was dressed in costumes. I knew you felt bad but if I had taken £40 and bought you a costume, what would we have eaten the next week or two? What would you have done with the costume after? I have to take everything into consideration. I can't always do what your friend's mum does. I hope you understand. I love you and would always try and do what's best for us.

My idea for writing this is to try and explain a bit about freedom and security as I see it. I hope what I've written will be of some help to you. My dream for you is that you try and be yourself at all times. Rise above mishaps, trials and temptation. Remember always, the best care one gets is what he or she takes of oneself.

I'm A Storyteller

The art of storytelling has been around since time began. From the royal courts of Africa to the smallest of villages in rural England, storytellers were held in the highest esteem. They were the early news carriers that brought information in verse, music and dance.

The worth of being told a story, whether it be from a book or spoken should not be underestimated. This is especially true of children. Most children love stories, whether they are shared in the family or whispered to them in a corridor. Stories not only open up a child's imagination but they also impart knowledge, culture and heritage. Hearing a story is shown to develop a child's reading, writing, speech and listening skills.

We all can learn something from a story and in a way we are all storytellers of one kind or another.

No Bring E Ya

by Anita Allen.

No Bring E Ya

Mamma: *"Hey, stop, no bring e ya."*

Anita: *"Who! Wha?"*

Mamma: *"Nat wha, who"*

Me look back and a couldn't see a ting.

She said, *"Carry e back right now."*

"Who?" I still ask

"Listen to me," she said *"Go back to the dead house, walk around the coffin, stand for a short while, then come back."*

I was confused but I did as I was told.

Mamma: "Anita"

Anita: "Yes, Mam"

Mamma: "Make sure you don't say a word."

My friend Ellen had been very sick with jaundice as we used to call it. I now believe she had sickle cell. She died in the hospital and her body was taken to their family home. The afternoon of the funeral, some children from our class went to view the body. It was a real occasion.

I left the house with another friend. We walked all the way back. As I approached my home, my mother came to the road side and said to me,

"Carry e right back now."

I stood dead in my tracks for her face was so stern I thought I was about to get a beating.

So I asked *"Wha! Who?"*

She said, *"Ellen."*

I said *"Ellen is dead."*

But she said, *"When you left, you told your friend come lay a we go, and the spirit is following you."*

It was then I turned around, fearful as can be.

She said, *"Go straight back to the dead house, walk around the coffin, stand for a short while, then come straight back."*

On my way back I was still scared, I turned my shirt inside out and when I reached the door I walked backwards inside for fear she was still behind.

As fearful as I was that day, I never was afraid of Ellen because I always believed she was some place close to protect me.

79

Set of 8 original full colour posters.
2 pack sizes available - A2 or A3

For an order form please call Gatehouse Books on
0161 226 7152.

The posters reflect positive images of mothers and their children. Writing produced by the parent complements each poster. The collection supports the belief that parents are the first and most important teachers of a child.

Positive images of parents and children of African descent are rare. These posters will document, inspire and promote the value of families learning together and from each other.

The term 'parent' in the above instance applies equally to a child's carer or guardian.

Gatehouse Books

Gatehouse is a unique publisher
Our writers are adults who are developing their basic
reading and writing skills. Their ideas and experiences
make fascinating material for any reader, but are
particularly relevant for adults working on their reading
and writing skills. The writing strikes a chord – a shared
experience of struggling against many odds.

The format of our books is clear and uncluttered. The
language is familiar and the text is often line-broken, so
that each line ends at a natural pause.

Gatehouse books are both popular and respected within
Adult Basic Education throughout the English speaking
world. They are also a valuable resource within
secondary schools, Social Services and within the Prison
Education Service and Probation Services.

Booklist available

Gatehouse Books
Hulme Adult Education Centre
Stretford Road
Manchester
M15 5FQ.
Tel and Fax: 0161 226 7152
E-mail: office@gatehousebooks.org.uk
Website: www.gatehousebooks.org.uk

The Gatehouse Publishing Charity Ltd is a registered charity, no 1011042
Gatehouse Books Ltd is a company limited by guarantee reg. no. 2619614